MORE

RIDDLES

BY
BENNETT CERF

With Drawings by Roy McKie

BEGINNER BOOKS

A DIVISION OF RANDOM HOUSE, INC.

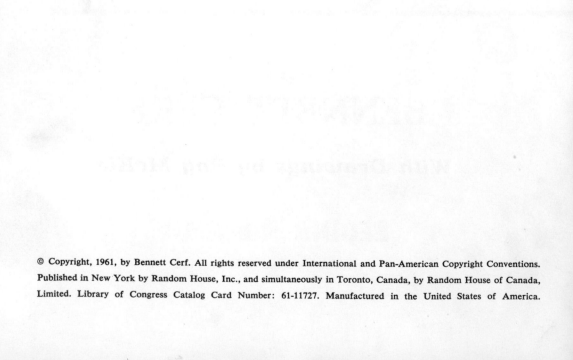

What is the best way
to get something out
from under an elephant?

Wait for the elephant
to go away.

For what man
should you always
take off your hat?

The barber.

Our hen can lay an egg

four inches long.

Can you beat that?

Yes. With an egg beater.

When can three big women
go out under one little umbrella
and not get wet?

When it is not raining.

When will a net
hold water?

When the water turns to ice.

What is the best way
to keep a skunk
from smelling?

Hold his nose.

What is the best way
to make pants last?

Make the coat first.

What is white,
has just one horn,
and gives milk?

A milk truck.

What is the best way
to catch a fish?

Have some one
throw it to you.

What kind of animal
eats with his tail?

All kinds of animals
eat with tails.
They can't take them off.

What is the hardest thing
about learning to ride
a bicycle?

The thing you fall on.

Why did the little boy
put ice in his father's bed?

Because he liked cold pop.

What sings,
has four legs,
is yellow, and
weighs 1,000 pounds?

Two 500 pound canaries.

What is the best thing
to put into a pie?

Your teeth.

What comes
all the way to a house,
but never gets in?

The steps.

When is a boy
not a boy?

When he turns into a store.

Why does a giraffe
eat so little?

Because a giraffe
can make a little
go a long way.

What horse can fly
like a bird?

A horsefly.

Why does a cook
always put on
a high white hat?

To cover his head.

What has . . .

Two legs like an Indian?

Two eyes like an Indian?

Two hands like an Indian?

Looks just like an Indian?

But is not an Indian?

A picture of an Indian.

What should you do
when you see a big lion?

Hope the big lion
does not see you.

What looks just like
half a loaf of bread?

The other half a loaf
of bread.

Can you drop a full glass
and spill no water?

Yes, when the glass
is full of milk.

Why does a cow
go over a hill?

Because a cow

can't go under a hill.

When should you give

elephant milk to a baby?

When the baby is an elephant.

What can fall down
and never get hurt?

Snow can fall down
and never get hurt.

Which will burn longer:
the candles on
the birthday cake of a boy,
        or
the candles on
the birthday cake of a girl?

No candles burn longer.

They all burn shorter.

Where will the cat be
when the lights go out?

In the dark.

What kind of coat
should be put on
when it is wet?

A coat of paint.

What bird can't fly as high
as you can jump?

A bird in a cage.

When should you put a saddle
on a horse backwards?

When you want to see
where you have been.